Stars Which See,
Stars Which Do Not
See

Books by Marvin Bell

Stars Which See, Stars Which Do Not See

POEMS BY

Marvin Bell

New York

Atheneum

1977

Acknowledgments are due the following books and periodicals
in whose pages these poems previously appeared:

THE AMERICAN POETRY ANTHOLOGY (AVON BOOKS): *Acceptance Speech.*
THE AMERICAN POETRY REVIEW: *After the Ducks Went In, By Different
    Paths, The Great South Bay, The Self and the Mulberry, To
    His Solitary Reader, To No One in Particular, Two Pictures of a Leaf,
    Whatever We Were Going to Tell Each Other Won't Mean As Much*
    and *Written During Depression: How to Be Happy.*
ANTAEUS: *Acceptance Speech, An Introduction to My Anthology* and
    Trinket.
THE ATLANTIC MONTHLY: *To Dorothy.*
CHICAGO REVIEW: *The House in Town* and *What Is There.*
THE FACE OF POETRY (GALLIMAUFRY): *Trinket.*
FIELD: *Gemwood.*
THE IOWA REVIEW: *A Goldfinch, Bits and Pieces of Our Land, John
    Clare's Badger* and *The Wild Cherry Tree Out Back.*
MISSISSIPPI REVIEW: *Three Parts Mud.*
THE NATION: *Dew at the Edge of a Leaf, "Gradually, It Occurs to
    Us . . . ", Lightning, Spenser, Chaucer, Dryden, Johnson, Browning,
    Tennyson, Dickens, Hardy and Kipling* and *Two Men in Wool Caps
    Catching Beaver.*
THE NEW YORKER: *The Mystery of Emily Dickinson, The Poem* and *Stars
    Which See, Stars Which Do Not See.*
THE OHIO REVIEW: *A Fish: On Beauty, Others Stop Elsewhere, The
    Great American Search for the Perfect Home Town* and *Unable to
    Wake in the Heat.*
POETRY: *New Students.*
POETRY AS PROCESS: ASK THE POET (DAVID MCKAY): *Gemwood.*
POETRY ON THE BUSES (PITTSBURGH): *An Elm We Lost.*
THE SENECA REVIEW: *A Catch of Weakfish from Peconic Bay.*
THE VIRGINIA QUARTERLY REVIEW: *Fresh News from the Past* and *Watching
    the Bomber Pass Over.*

Library of Congress Cataloging in Publication Data

Bell, Marvin.
    Stars which see, stars which do not see.
    I. Title.
PS3552.E52S7   811'.5'4   76–39922
ISBN 0–689–10779–X

To Nathan and Jason

Contents

1

The Poem

Would you like me more
if I were a woman?
Would you treat me better
were I a man?
I am just words, no
not words even, just marks
on a page, tokens of what?
Oh, you know.
Then tell them, will you.
Tell them to stop looking for me.
Tell them I never left home.
Tell them, if you must,
that I never left my body.
Unlike so many others,
I had no wings, just shoulders.
I was, like the snow bunting,
of stout build but moderate size.
Better make that "exceedingly" moderate size.
I neither blessed nor cursed
but that the good suffered
and evil closed the books in triumph.
I cured no one.
When I died, my bones
turned to dust, not diamonds.
At best, a tooth or two became coal.
How long it took.
You would have liked me then,
had you been alive still.
Had you survived
the silliness of the self,
you would have treated me better.
I never lied to you,
once I had grown up.

When x told you you were wonderful,
I said only that you existed.
When y said that you were awful,
I said only that life continues.
I did not mean a life like yours.
Not life so proud to be life.
Not life so conscious of life.
Not life reduced to this life or that life.
Not life as something—to see or own.
Not life as a form of life
which wants wings it doesn't have
and a skeleton of jewels,
not this one of bones and becoming.
How perfect are my words now,
in your absence!
Ungainly yet mild perhaps,
taking the place of no field,
offering neither to stand in the place of a tree
nor where the water was,
neither under your heel nor floating,
just gradually appearing,
gainless and insubstantial,
near you as always,
asking you to dance.

The Self and the Mulberry

I wanted to see the self, so I looked at the mulberry.
It had no trouble accepting its limits,
yet defining and redefining a small area
so that any shape was possible, any movement.
It stayed put, but was part of all the air.
I wanted to learn to be there and not there
like the continually changing, slightly moving
mulberry, wild cherry and particularly the willow.
Like the willow, I tried to weep without tears.
Like the cherry tree, I tried to be sturdy and productive.
Like the mulberry, I tried to keep moving.
I couldn't cry right, couldn't stay or go.
I kept losing parts of myself like a soft maple.
I fell ill like the elm. That was the end
of looking in nature to find a natural self.
Let nature think itself not manly enough!
Let nature wonder at the mystery of laughter.
Let nature hypothesize man's indifference to it.
Let nature take a turn at saying what love is!

Unable to Wake in the Heat

I can hold up my head, if barely.
Parts of the body reassemble
as in a middle movement of Brahms.
At the porch screens, large ferns
try to brush away the summer spiders.
They go on combing the muggy air
because they are strong and wide,
but the tiger-lilies droop their heads
and the willow, always a leaner,
shakes her long hair in a slow dance.

There is a wonderful hallucination
in this—the consciousness of not waking,
the dimness, the weight of the body.
The head weighs the most, unbearably heavy,
and the eyes are like steel under blankets.
The head falls, finally, to the chest,
the back of the neck numb with straining,
but we know we could go even further.
We hear music far back in our not-knowing.
Our faces relax: nothing odd there.

The Mystery of Emily Dickinson

Sometimes the weather goes on for days
but you were different. You were divine.
While the others wrote more and longer,
you wrote much more and much shorter.
I held your white dress once: 12 buttons.
In the cupola, the wasps struck glass
as hard to escape as you hit your sound
again and again asking Welcome. No one.

Except for you, it were a trifle:
This morning, not much after dawn,
in level country, not New England's,
through leftovers of summer rain I
went out rag-tag to the curb, only
a sleepy householder at his routine
bending to trash, when a young girl
in a white dress your size passed,

so softly!, carrying her shoes. It must be
she surprised me—her barefoot quick-step
and the earliness of the hour, your dress—
or surely I'd have spoken of it sooner.
I should have called to her, but a neighbor
wore that look you see against happiness.
I won't say anything would have happened
unless there was time, and eternity's plenty.

Trinket

I love watching the water
ooze through the crack in the fern pot,
it's a small thing

that slows time
and steadies
and gives me ideas of becoming

having nothing to do
with ambition or even reaching,
it isn't necessary at such times

to describe this,
it's no image for mean keeping,
it's no thing that small

but presence.
Other men look at the ocean,
and I do too,

though it is too many
presences for any
to absorb.

It's this other,
a little water, used, appearing
slowly around the sounds

of oxygen and small frictions,
that gives the self
the notion of the self

one is always losing
until these tiny embodiments
small enough to contain it.

The Wild Cherry Tree Out Back

The leaves are kites.
What are their goals?

In snow and sun
it files upwards—to where?

It more than fills
the painting one might have made.

It shadows and shrinks
the person who might have stood

beneath its reaching.
It seems to make its own light.

Let me be like that tree,
one might have said,

before the carving
had come far from the wood,

before the map was a shoe
and the branches were made oars.

That was before
we could piss in a drawer,

when snow and sun were tact,
the tree too personal for words.

Let me be like that tree,
putting to rest

the spring
and wandering.

Two Pictures of a Leaf

If I make up this leaf
in the shape of a fan, the day's cooler
and drier than any tree. But if
under a tree I place before me
this same leaf as on a plate,
dorsal side up and then its ribs
set down like the ribs of a fish—
then I know that fish are dead to us
from the trees, and the leaf
sprawls in the net of fall to be
boned and eaten while the wind gasps.
Ah then, the grounds are a formal ruin
whereon the lucky who lived
come to resemble so much that does not.

Lightning

The roots of the tree are elastic, but
the huge elm wants to become
a cathedral—in a second more sudden,
more sudden than faith!—
which might have happened in just
such an instant: following the sign from the sky,
a homing flash and then
halves where there was one (tree, mind, way
of thinking, feeling). To contain a cathedral,

a tree must be very large, larger
than most. This one has the look of
a great event, a rupture (crusaders
could pray here), but *in*
reality, it has only the split personality
of the wooden saviour.

This is the present. Earlier,
I loved that old violin for winds, that tree,
that (like me) unpolished ladder
to this or that fine something I'll never see,
gone now to music.

An Elm We Lost

On it we wrote a little essay
about who loved who.
Shade moves in the grass, never still,
and they still do.

Stars Which See, Stars Which Do Not See

They sat by the water. The fine women
had large breasts, tightly checked.
At each point, at every moment,
they seemed happy by the water.
The women wore hats like umbrellas
or carried umbrellas shaped like hats.
The men wore no hats and the water,
which wore no hats, had that well-known
mirror finish which tempts sailors.
Although the men and women seemed at rest
they were looking toward the river
and some way out into it but not beyond.
The scene was one of hearts and flowers
though this may be unfair. Nevertheless,
it was probable that the Seine had hurt them,
that they were "taken back" by its beauty
to where a slight breeze broke the mirror
and then its promise, but never the water.

2

To No One in Particular

Whether you sing or scream,
the process is the same.
You start, inside yourself,
a small explosion, the difference
being that in the scream
the throat is squeezed so that
the back of the tongue
can taste the brain's fear.
Also, spittle and phlegm
are components of the instrument.
I guess it would be possible
to take someone by the throat
and give him a good beating.
All the while, though, some fool
would be writing down the notes
of the victim, underscoring
this phrase, lightening this one,
adding a grace note and a trill
and instructions in one of those languages
revered for its vowels.
But all the time, it's consonants
coming from the throat.
Here's the one you were throttling,
still gagging out the guttural ch—
the throat-clearing, Yiddish ch—
and other consonants spurned by
opera singers and English teachers.
He won't bother you again.
He'll scrape home to take it out
on his wife, more bestial consonants
rising in pitch until spent.
Then he'll lock a leg over her
and snore, and all the time

he hasn't said a word we can repeat.
Even though we all speak his language.
Even though the toast in our throats
in the morning has a word for us—
not at all like bread in rain,
but something grittier in something
thicker, going through what we are.
Even though we snort and sniffle,
cough, hiccup, cry and come
and laugh until our stomachs turn.
Who will write down this language?
Who will do the work necessary?
Who will gag on a chickenbone
for observation? Who will breathe perfectly
under water? Whose slow murder
will disprove for all time
an alphabet meant to make sense?
Listen! I speak to you in one tongue,
but every moment that ever mattered to me
occurred in another language.
Starting with my first word.
To no one in particular.

Acceptance Speech

My friends,
I am amazed

to be Professor
in a University

seven times larger
than my home town

and all because
I went away. Meanwhile,

the roots of the ivy
just went on crawling

in the dirt in the dark,
the light that was Brady's

and Gardner's during
our Civil War

became the blaze
in Southeast Asia

and soon everywhere
men lay down

without their women
which is what can happen

when people like me
leave home hoping

to be promoted
and end up promoted

to the rank of Captain
and discharged honorably

just before
whatever new war

we should always have known
was always coming

out of torn pockets and salt
from needles and patches of flowers

out of places for lost birds
night fog and a dying moon

from the work we do yea
(death being

what we don't do).
So to be at work

offending death
which others welcomed

who left home too
and no differently

seems to me half
of a famous story

I have never read
even in school.

New Students

Old already? —Provable still.
The stars walk home with us after class.
They are on their way somewhere too—
all ways to timelessness, as we
are on our way to thoughtlessness.

The moon says Folly to explain. Explain,
Moon, folly and profound thoughtlessness.

Ok, the moon says, or whatever we want
it to say: there's a way in which you are loved,

an anatomy of correspondence, and
a shapeless universe disguised as time—
which is not possible to understand.
That is why this circumstance of energy
is recorded as glory and passes into study.

A Fish: On Beauty

The catfish I'd caught was more whiskery
than whiskery, bigger than big enough.
The hammer that built the toolbox
was barely enough: it dotted its skull
like a cane impresses a carpet
and the blows repeated its life
half a dozen times before the end.

There was that detective in the story,
cornering the suspect, turned his revolver
in his hand and hammered the butt-end
against all protestations of innocence.
Artful, the way the author told it.
That catfish was ugly, I think.
The longer it took, the uglier he got.

After the Ducks Went In

We picked up eggs
and ducks. Some were sicker
than medicine, or the cost of it.
Weaklings, they lay on their sides.
They lifted their heads less and less.
Ducks are dumb
but even a duck has better sense
than to die. So I swung each
small contagion by its feet
against a tree till its neck broke.

I went far away to schoolroom *ethics*,
where too many were in
the lifeboat in the textbook.
Whom to toss out? The optimists
looked up everywhere, the pessimists
nowhere or down to let it happen.
Well, I could have broken my own neck
instead of those ducks'. Ethics
is not what you think.
Our class-conscience is clear. They all drowned.

Written During Depression: How to Be Happy

To be happy,
a man must love death
and failure. Then,
however great the flash
of this moment or that bit
of life's work, there
will come always another moment
to be appreciated because
fading or crumbling. If,
however, a man loves
life, there can be no end to it,
nor hope. If a man loves
reason, eventually he
will find none. If he loves
the interest of others,
he will be made to apologize
continually for his own being.
If he loves form, all
that he does or knows will
come, not to nothing, but
to that other possibility
of meaninglessness: everything.
That is why "the shape of things
to come" is a phrase littered with
tracks into the bush
where the pure primitive
is a headhunter's delusion,
and why, my dear, I love you.

Spenser, Chaucer, Dryden, Johnson, Browning, Tennyson, Dickens, Hardy and Kipling

Ladies and gentlemen,
the English language
holds in the hearts of
each of you a place
where the poets lie buried
in a musty community.
Here is that place.

Think not of Shakespeare!
He's off by himself.
That's what he gets
for a girl at Court
and a wife in the suburbs,
and talking so common.
He had to go home.

London's no bargain
for those who remain.
We came in the rain
and left it to rain,
Madame's wax faces
perfect and the Commonwealth
compounding ruin.

Don't anybody bury
Whitman and Williams,
and seven as American
in one stony Corner,—
and the rest of us neither.
Death is no anthology,
or a cough in the audience.

We all know how many times
a critic reads a book:
less than once. So if we
have to be buried alive,
let those who always know better
look for us one at a time
in the ground gone over.

"Gradually, It Occurs to Us . . ."

Gradually, it occurs to us
that none of it was necessary—
not the heavy proclaiming
the sweat and length of our love
when, together, we thought it the end;
nor the care we gave your dress,
smoothing it as we would the sky;
nor the inevitable envelope of This-
is-the-time-we-always-knew-would-come,
and-goodbye. All that was ever needed
was all that we had to offer,
and we have had it all. I have your absence.
And have left myself inside you.
Now when you come back to me,
or I to you, don't give it a thought.
This time, when first we fall into bed,
we won't know who we are, or where,
or what is going to happen to us.
Time is memory. We have the time.

Two Men in Wool Caps Catching Beaver

Home is a white sheet of a tent
strung to elms, and a stovepipe
come through up to an elbow.
From a peg where the door folds
a revolver hangs by its trigger guard.
Six skins are spaced along a line
while two fresh kills hang on a tree.

Sometimes, you think you know what people
think of you, and it's not much.
Then you have your picture taken.
Someone takes your photo in the sunlight
locking their elbows so that the trees
behind you come out sharp and even
the pleats at the corners of your eyes.

No one can say now you didn't laugh.
You were warm nights and kept by
a lantern. You knew how to preserve
whatever you wanted to save, lived on,
and protected your head. Now people
wear hats for looks, but yours had the
only style that matters: concern elsewhere.

3

The Great South Bay

froze, hardest winters,
from Center Moriches to Fire Island.
Two could bounce-pass a basketball
to measure the distance across
in warmth. Nearby, the ice boats
marked off their formal pleasures
in great slicing swoops with no warmth
but all that speed water-locked.

Over the thin stretch of Fire Island
once ours, there came a mad wind
and then ocean, like mad tongues trying
to tell us to take cover. Many did.
Remembering the hurricane of my first year,
when boats beached on our lawn,
and no tree was sure in its place—
remembering, I went as far as police

toward that water-targeted strip
of sand, where homes on stilts would not
be high enough again (there was a place
to cross by land, in a rich town)
and there I stood to watch, longer than dare,
the real state and status of water,
an ocean's worth at a stone's throw (but
how remembered?) till they turned me back.

A Catch of Weakfish from Peconic Bay

Every one of them was caught mouth first—
a moral lesson, no? This town stopped
thirteen trains in 1937. Any morning
commuters rode on running boards
last-minute to the station.
There was always someone.

No industry to speak of. Evenings,
they all came back to the fish.
Now fish swim in schools and know a lot.
Twenty-eight have been landed by four.
The fish are lined up. The men are lined up.
They look on Long Island like many.

We might say they look like the past
or childhood, where the trains stopped.
But no. This catch of fish is instructive,
if you care. If not, you might not notice
the rural faces, or that those who lived
the longest are at the ends of the line.

John Clare's Badger

The man we had thought drunk
was twice-stabbed, and the knife
left in his back. I remember
his falling forward, or not one of us
would have come down from the fence.

We would sit that fence at dusk
and truckloads of potatoes, ducks
and cauliflower spill on past
and the farmers without a whimper.
Salt air came up the street

from the South. East and time past
New Amsterdam, we faced
the Atlantic and (we knew this) England.
We were not called. Not chosen.
England might have been a star.

You want to know what happened
to that man? He lived. He fought back.
He's going to die. If there's a reason
it took these twenty years
to round him up again, that may be why.

Fresh News from the Past

Many were happy.
It took a long time to make a wish.
Daffodils were trampled in play
and clover ripped up
by hands feeling for luck.
Ivy wouldn't stop.

There was a kind of weed made spinners
and a best grass reed
for making the hands a wind instrument.
No one who had seen Queen Anne's lace
knew it. There was suitable weather.
There was a road under the river.

Had we been to Paris? No,
but we had been to leg-of-lamb
and found it alive and moving.
Guns-and-butter had not yet become
rockets-and-pies. We were dumb
as ducks. We loved the word "propellor."

Three Parts Mud

1

One thing: I found a feather
stuck there, a wing-feather showing
plenty of blue with a white tip.
Usually, the mud arrives
with permissions of warm air.
Formerly, the blue jay
depended on his rights, but this
is safer, and luckier if
a sparrow's near.

2

We threw a mouse
in the clay-making vat—not so
good as a one-hundred-year-old Chinese
village pit. But his bones enriched
our pottery, and took in the kiln
their own flag of cremation.
In the glaze, a personal touch.
In the silt of the nearby
Wapsipinicon, clay enough.

3

John is dead, but I
stand on the deck of his rough clammer,
and see still the bird that left
a nest and feather, and wrongs
the clay made right.
Fragments, mud kept them all—
a kind of money for most people:
those that have trouble,
or used to.

To His Solitary Reader

If once he slept with Donne
(happily) now he sleeps

with Williams,
the old Williams.

The *being*
we have and do

is not what we "are."
Memory is what we are,

where they
think they know us!

The self moves too fast
for company.

The self never doubts
what the self needs, of course!

The inexhaustible accommodation
of the public self

while not altogether
serious in any sense,

encrusts us—witness
a fossil, unknown,

in the thunder stone
rolled over ages

to a beach in Seattle,
not now to be broken.

The heavy *being* inside
must be tiny. The rock's

the weight.
This is evidence:

an argument to the particular
from the general,

backwards
from what you think.

Time's determinant.
Once, I knew you.

What Is There

When the grass, wet and matted,
is thick as a dry lawn is not,
I think of a kind of printing—
a page at a time, and the thick
paper hung up to dry, its
deep impressions filled and shapely
where ink is held and hardens.

And I wonder then at the underside
of those damp sheets of grass—
the muddy blood of those buried
coming up into the flattened green
as I press it underfoot, and pass,
and the sun drawing moisture
until we accept what is written there.

Dew at the Edge of a Leaf

The broader leaves collect
enough to see early
by a wide spread of moonlight,
and they shine!, shine!—
who are used to turning
faces to the light.

Looking up is farthest.
From here or under any tree,
I know what will transpire:
leaves in their watery halos have
an overhead-to-underfoot career,
and thrive toward falling.

In a passage of time and water,
I am half-way—a leaf in July?
In August? I take no pity.
Everything green is turning brown,
it's true, but then too
everything turning brown is green!

By Different Paths

We have all had our heads in a book
on the trouble with love
or, say, by a river looking for answers
downstream we have come to a place
somewhere inside us as smooth as
the guarded heart of an acorn
and how we came to be lost so
completely to one feeling
no one can say.

Ah, rules: of trees toward light
and water, cork and dead men to the surface,
some would say lunatics to the fringes.
But you and I, by different paths,
have arrived upstream from many possible
replies—I hope a craggy surface
won't prevent you—and the deaths we drop
stay down, lightheadedness also.
Now love is easy, pleases; no answer.

Whatever We Were Going to Tell Each Other Won't Mean As Much

You were brushing your hair.
Interminably, you brushed your soft hair.
How could you know what it was doing to me?
You knew. You kept brushing your hair.

I watched. I watched. I turned away,
hearing the sound of your hairbrush
soften as your hair found its place,
very like the sound of a rough hand on a dress.

How could you know I went on listening?
You knew. Even when you were finished,
you kept on brushing. Even when it was over,
you kept on brushing. You knew. You knew.

4

An Introduction to My Anthology

Such a book must contain—
it always does!—a disclaimer.
I make no such. For here
I have collected all the best—
the lily from the field among them,
forget-me-nots and mint weed,
a rose for whoever expected it,
and a buttercup for the children
to make their noses yellow.

Here is clover for the lucky
to roll in, and milkweed to clatter,
a daisy for one judgment,
and a violet for when he loves you
or if he loves you not and why not.
Those who sniff and say no,
These are the wrong ones (and
there always are such people!)—
let them go elsewhere, and quickly!

For you and I, who have made it this far,
are made happy by occasions
requiring orchids, or queenly arrangements
and even a bird of paradise,
but happier still by the flowers of
circumstance, cattails of our youth,
field grass and bulrush. I have included
the devil's paint-brush
but only as a peacock among barn fowl.

A Goldfinch

The Baltimore oriole, seldom an Iowan,
was last thought seen to be bathing
where we took coffee on a sweltering morning
yet in Iowa, a fan failing at our feet.
It was a sign, not of betrayal either.
That yellow breast of hers looked cool
and the white bars on her black wings
returned to us the formal in weather
without shape, shimmery. So a goldfinch.
The mind is a wonder, is my summary.

Others Stop Elsewhere

Half past the Midwest, going West,
we let ourselves say mid-praise
for such as we had seen.
They had seen it, but farther on:
a form in the wilderness—
face of a nation, or maybe beast.

Some went on. We returned,
stopping slowly. Once in our state
a glacier stopped—that
was an event!—and made the land
mean something more,
forming here. Now it is warmer.

Descendants of theirs go by us,
speeding up toward wilder forms,
riding on our shapes in the earth.
If truth has to go on forever,
that glacier isn't true. But it's true.
For us, this was the place to be stopping.

The Great American Search for the Perfect Home Town

Sometimes the land was water,
sometimes land. Anyone American
from Lincoln can earn
what someone, say, in Defiance

Ohio wants paid. When we came
to the place we live
those were wisest who had lived
there longest, and we were not

wise at all. Now they are wiser
still and we are just the same:
lucky. When we say "this Thanksgiving,"
the reference of this is that.

The House in Town

The kind of expert I like's
a friend—the birds know, up top
crossing lines and mixing phrases
till the air's a foray of whole notes
(ragged by a standard that's wrong).

What's the best that ever happened
to us? We'd need all the notes
to say it, to make it happen
again the way the birds remember,
the day the family that stayed

moved into our house, a hundred
years (and more) of wood and plaster
under the two doomed double elms.
Eight years later, we're specialists
at moving in.

I could say more. The birds, though,
say what they said then.
The distance in a greeting is
what the greeting means, the birds say,—
who leave out a lot they *could* say.

Bits and Pieces of Our Land

One day you will put it together
the way they do the world
in the globe shop.

Meanwhile, you can see:
the compass plant points to the barnswallow
and a piece of prairie

might edge the road. In your mind,
no state bird, no tree,
but finch and sparrow cluster

in willow, ash, or hardwood
here and there; then,
others, elsewhere.

It's not that the land can't
make up its mind
to be a place for grass or bush,

timber or rock. The land thinks
by watching you look around;
in its stopped-down time

it will become what you want it
to be, and then become
all that it wanted you to.

It is something to see:
the way it is turning us over
in your thoughts or mine.

Watching the Bomber Pass Over

How can we speak of eyes and seasons
(or a tree-sore in the shape of a horse-collar)
when the eyes are yanked upwards
and the lightest season made thicker
by the indifference of its metal?
And that is not everything, for in
the time it takes to start a wind,
this romance of progress, this story
of wings, this monstrous dare,
can be brought crushingly to earth.

How can we bend to the nibbled bark
of the sapling, and fence round
the wind-torn and weeping bushes,
when the moon which was our candy father
is a stone's throw and a dry station?
How stake tomatoes and thin the lettuce
when war is a question of permission,
and the history of the human passion
is written by a clock seeking a promotion,
and History loves Hitler, not Schweitzer?

You know the way the water for flowers
passes them by and remains a while below
and then is slowly drawn upwards
lighter for the settling, leaving its grit,
without which it would never have fallen,
to the soil: well, that is the way it is.
Grief falls everywhere. How joyful we are!
Around us spring up lives like ours,
not one of us has all the cares of the world!,
not one of us escapes some little happiness!

To Dorothy

You are not beautiful, exactly.
You are beautiful, inexactly.
You let a weed grow by the mulberry
and a mulberry grow by the house.
So close, in the personal quiet
of a windy night, it brushes the wall
and sweeps away the day till we sleep.

A child said it, and it seemed true:
"Things that are lost are all equal."
But it isn't true. If I lost you,
the air wouldn't move, nor the tree grow.
Someone would pull the weed, my flower.
The quiet wouldn't be yours. If I lost you,
I'd have to ask the grass to let me sleep.

Gemwood

to Nathan and Jason, our sons

In the *shoppes*
they're showing "gemwood":
the buffed-up flakes of dye-fed pines—
bright concentrics or bull's-eyes,
wide-eyed on the rack of
this newest "joint effort
of man and nature." But then

those life-lines circling
each target chip of "gemwood"
look less like eyes, yours or mine,
when we have watched a while.
They are more like the whorls
at the tips of our fingers,
which no one can copy. Even on

the photocopy Jason made of
his upraised hands, palms down
to the machine, they do not appear.
His hands at five-years-old—
why did we want to copy them, and
why does the grey yet clear print
make me sad? That summer,

the Mad River followed us
through Vermont—a lusher state than
our own. A thunderous matinee
of late snows, and then the peak
at Camel's Hump was bleached.
As a yellow pear is to the sky—
that was our feeling. We had with us

a rat from the lab—no, a pet
we'd named, a pure friend who changed
our minds. When it rained near
the whole of the summer, in that
cabin Nathan made her a social creature.
She was all our diversion, and brave.
That's why, when she died

in the heat of our car
one accidental day we didn't intend,
it hurt her master first and most,
being his first loss like that,
and the rest of our family felt badly
even to tears, for a heart that small.
We buried her by the road

in the Adirondack Mountains,
and kept our way to Iowa.
Now it seems to me the heart
must enlarge to hold the losses
we have ahead of us. I hold to
a certain sadness the way others
search for joy, though I like joy.

Home, sunlight cleared the air
and all the green's of consequence. Still
when it ends, we won't remember
that it ended. If parents must receive
the sobbing, that is nothing
when put next to the last crucial fact
of who is doing the crying.

Marvin Bell

Marvin Bell was born August 3, 1937 in New York
City, and grew up in Center Moriches, on the south
shore of eastern Long Island. He now lives in Iowa
City, where he teaches for The University of Iowa. For
his poetry he has received the Lamont Award of The
Academy of American Poets, the Bess Hokin Award
from *Poetry*, an Emily Clark Balch Prize from *The
Virginia Quarterly Review* and a Guggenheim Fellowship.